100
Bible
Verses

Publications International, Ltd.

1

Trust in the Lord with all thine heart; and lean not unto thine own understanding.
In all thy ways acknowledge him, and he shall direct thy paths.
—Proverbs 3:5–6

I can look over my shoulder and see times when you, Pathfinding God, were a ready and dependable companion. I couldn't have done it without you. And I believe that you are already waiting to take my hand into tomorrow—knowledge that gives me the security to take risks.

2

How great are his signs! and how mighty are his wonders! his kingdom is an everlasting kingdom, and his dominion is from generation to generation.
—Daniel 4:3

Regardless of what the future holds, I'm savoring all sorts of wondrous things I've been too busy to notice before. A thousand daily marvels bring a smile to my face. Through your grace, Lord, rather than thinking how sad it is that I missed them before, I'm delighted to be seeing and doing them now. These small wonders energize me, and for that I'm thankful. It's never too late to be a joyful explorer.

3

Lead me in thy truth, and teach me: for thou art the God of my salvation; on thee do I wait all the day.
—Psalm 25:5

Life has made the most hopeful among us skeptical, Lord of truth. Much is bogus, making us uncertain. Thank you for the gift of doubt, for it sparks our seeking. Keep us lively and excited as we set off on quests blessed by you, heeding your advice to knock, seek, and ask.

4

Who is he that condemneth? It is Christ that died, yea rather, that is risen again, who is even at the right hand of God, who also maketh intercession for us.
—Romans 8:34

Lord, how unworthy we feel of your son's prayers on our behalf, but how grateful we are for his intercession! It's all more marvelous, more mysterious than we can grasp, but because we trust your Word and your heart, we humbly thank him for caring so much about us. Surely his prayers are heard above all others!

5

Heal me, O Lord, and I shall be healed; save me,
and I shall be saved: for thou art my praise.
—Jeremiah 17:14

Lord, bless all those today who need healing of any kind.
Whether it be physical, emotional, or mental, bless them with
your merciful grace and eternal love. Let each one know that
they are special in your eyes and that, in the realm of spirit,
there is only perfection, wholeness, and joy. Amen.

6

A friend loveth at all times, and a brother is born for adversity.
—Proverbs 17:17

People can often sense when someone is in need of prayer—
even if that someone is miles away. If the thought of a friend
should come into your mind, why not stop and say a little
prayer on their behalf?

7

Not rendering evil for evil, or railing for railing: but
contrariwise blessing; knowing that ye are thereunto called,
that ye should inherit a blessing.
—1 Peter 3:9

Let's revive the custom of blessing. When we bless someone,
we show love and respect. Sincerely honoring the people and
things in our lives is a wonderful way of showing gratitude to
the Lord.

8

Wherefore, if God so clothe the grass of the field, which to day is, and to morrow is cast into the oven, shall he not much more clothe you, O ye of little faith?
Therefore take no thought, saying, What shall we eat? or, What shall we drink? or, Wherewithal shall we be clothed?
—Matthew 6:30–31

If I count the things I've asked for that you have not given me, I begin to believe you do not love me, God. But if, instead, I bring to mind all of the goodness you have shown me, I come to trust that you have never given me less than what I need and often have blessed me with far more from a depth of love I cannot comprehend.

9

Whosoever therefore shall humble himself as this little child, the same is greatest in the kingdom of heaven.
—Matthew 18:4

Bless the children, God of little ones, with their giggles and wide-eyed awe, their assumption that today will be chock-full of surprises, learning, and love. Neither missing nor wasting a minute, they take nothing for granted. Their example blesses us. We will go and do likewise.

10

Let us therefore come boldly unto the throne of grace, that we may obtain mercy, and find grace to help in time of need.
—Hebrews 4:16

Everything looks much brighter than it did before. My prayer for strength has been answered. My cries for help have been heard. My pleas for mercy flew directly to your throne. Now I'm ready to help my neighbor, Lord. Let me not delay.

11

The Lord is my rock, and my fortress, and my deliverer; my God, my strength, in whom I will trust; my buckler, and the horn of my salvation, and my high tower.
—Psalm 18:2

Lord, you are the foundation of my life. When circumstances shift and make my world unsteady, you remain firm. When threats of what lies ahead blow against the framework of my thoughts, you are solid. When I focus on your steadfastness, I realize that you are my strength for the moment, the one sure thing in my life. Because of you I stand now, and I will stand tomorrow as well, because you are there already. Amen.

12

But the fruit of the Spirit is love, joy, peace, longsuffering, gentleness, goodness, faith, meekness, temperance: against such there is no law.
—Galatians 5:22–23

Thank you, Father, for your Holy Spirit, who guides me through each day. Help me to obey quickly when I am asked to serve or forgive others. May I always be thankful and rejoice in the blessings pointed out to me along the way.

13

And there ye shall eat before the Lord your God, and ye shall rejoice in all that ye put your hand unto, ye and your households, wherein the Lord thy God hath blessed thee.
—Deuteronomy 12:7

May you find joy and satisfaction in your family life. In building a home and setting up a residence—be blessed! In finding a job and working diligently—be blessed! In taking care of little ones and making friends in the neighborhood—be blessed! In seeking God for all your help and guidance, bringing every care to him, yes, may you indeed be blessed.

14

And the Lord God formed man of the dust of the ground, and breathed into his nostrils the breath of life; and man became a living soul.
—Genesis 2:7

Lord, with each breath I take I am aware that it is you who breathed life into me. My next breath is as dependent on you as my last breath was. And I can confidently rest in the knowledge that it will be you and you alone who will determine when the last breath leaves my body and I go to be with you. Today, Lord, I thank you for the gift of life and for each breath I take.

15

Be careful for nothing; but in every thing by prayer and supplication with thanksgiving let your requests be made known unto God.
—Philippians 4:6

Prayer, O God, is as steadying as a hand on the rudder of a free-floating boat and as reliable as sunrise after night. It keeps me going, connected as I am to you, the source of wind beneath my daily wings.

16

And walk in love, as Christ also hath loved us, and hath given himself for us an offering and a sacrifice to God for a sweetsmelling savour.
—Ephesians 5:2

God, you gave up your own beloved son for me. How could I possibly love with such a sense of sacrifice? Help me be the kind of person who can put the needs of others before my own. Help me give until it hurts. You have sacrificed for me—now let me give of myself in return. I know that in the end, I will be rewarded with your merciful grace. Amen.

17

And I will bring the blind by a way that they knew not; I will lead them in paths that they have not known: I will make darkness light before them, and crooked things straight. These things will I do unto them, and not forsake them.
—Isaiah 42:16

Lord, how grateful I am that you are willing to go before me to prepare the way. Even when I sense that a new opportunity is from you and has your blessing, I've learned I still need to stop and ask you to lead before I take the first step. Otherwise I will stumble along in the dark tripping over stones of my own creation! Everything goes more smoothly when you are involved, Lord.

18

If any of you lack wisdom, let him ask of God, that giveth to all men liberally, and upbraideth not; and it shall be given him.
—James 1:5

Thank you for your wise ways, Lord. Following them fills my life with true blessings—the riches of love and relationship, joy and provision, peace and protection. I remember reading in your Word that whenever I ask for your wisdom from a faith-filled heart, you will give it, no holds barred. So I'll ask once again today for your insight and understanding as I build, using your blueprints.

19

But godliness with contentment is great gain.
—1 Timothy 6:6

I celebrate the gift of contentment, knowing there is no guarantee it will last. But for now, it's great to rest—just rest—in this wonderful calm.

20

Judge not, and ye shall not be judged: condemn not, and ye shall not be condemned: forgive, and ye shall be forgiven.
—Luke 6:37

I pray, Lord, for the ability to learn forgiveness. Often within my heart there is much that is negative. I pray to learn to let go of those feelings. I pray to learn to forgive others as I wish to be forgiven. I pray for the gifts of understanding and compassion as I strive to be more like you. Amen.

21

Thy word is a lamp unto my feet, and a light unto my path.
—Psalm 119:105

Lord, in your infinite wisdom you knew we would need instruction for life, and so you placed in your Word the guidelines for living a productive life that brings you glory. Your Word nurtures us body and soul and keeps our minds focused on the beautiful, positive aspects of life. Thank you, Lord, for not leaving us here without a guidebook. We'd be lost without your Word.

22

Save me, O God; for the waters are come in unto my soul.
—Psalm 69:1

Just when all seems hopeless, prayer lifts us like a boat on an ocean wave. A sturdy craft, prayer doesn't hide from pain, but uses it like the force of the sea to move us to a new place of insight, patience, courage, and sympathy. Always, it is God's hand beneath the surface holding us up.

23

I will praise the name of God with a song, and will magnify him with thanksgiving.
—Psalm 69:30

Cherish the chance to work and play and think and speak and sing; all simple pleasures are opportunities for grateful praise.

24

Now faith is the substance of things hoped for, the evidence of things not seen.
—Hebrews 11:1

God of my life, though you are not visible to me, I see evidence of your existence everywhere I look. You speak to me in silent ways with an inaudible voice. How can I explain this mystery—what I know to be true but cannot prove? This spiritual sensitivity—this awareness of you—is more real to me than the pages on which my eyes fall at this moment. You exist, and I believe.

25

For I am persuaded that neither death, nor life, nor angels, nor principalities, nor powers, nor things present, nor things to come,
Nor height, nor depth, nor any other creature, shall be able to separate us from the love of God, which is in Christ Jesus our Lord.
—Romans 8:38–39

May you come to know that God is your friend. When you feel a frowning face is looking down at you from heaven, recall that nothing you could do could ever make God love you more or love you less. He simply loves—completely, perfectly. So feel the blessedness of that!

26

He maketh the storm a calm, so that the waves thereof
are still.
Then are they glad because they be quiet; so he bringeth
them unto their desired haven.
—Psalm 107:29–30

Sometimes my heart is so overwhelmed, God, that I don't
know where to begin my prayer. Help me to quiet my soul
and remember that you know everything inside of my mind
before I ever come to you with it. Still, I need to tell you about
it, Lord, and I know you want me to tell you. Thank you for
being such a faithful listener and for caring about everything
that concerns me. When I remember that, it helps me slow
down, take a deep breath, and begin the conversation.

27

Now there are diversities of gifts, but the same Spirit.
—1 Corinthians 12:4

Help me take stock of your gifts to me, Lord. I'm good at things that appear to be so insignificant. Chances are you can use any one of these gifts, no matter how simple they appear, to help others. Remind me that it's not what I do but my doing it that ultimately matters.

28

But I say unto you, Love your enemies, bless them that curse you, do good to them that hate you, and pray for them which despitefully use you, and persecute you.
—Matthew 5:44

Heavenly Father, give us the forgiving spirit we so badly need to heal the wounds of the past. Help us live "the better life" by making peace with our enemies and understanding that they, too, need your love. Amen.

29

For we know that if our earthly house of this tabernacle were dissolved, we have a building of God, an house not made with hands, eternal in the heavens.
—2 Corinthians 5:1

Lord, how hopelessly aware we are of our earthly bodies. They develop creaks and frailties—not to mention weird bumps and lumps! But thanks to you, we are so much more than our bodies. For although we live in the flesh, we are filled with your Holy Spirit; the life we live is really you living out your life in us! Thank you for that perspective, Lord. It makes it so much easier to watch our earthly bodies begin to fail. How ready we will be to exchange them for the heavenly models!

30

The Lord hath appeared of old unto me, saying, Yea, I have loved thee with an everlasting love: therefore with lovingkindness have I drawn thee.
—Jeremiah 31:3

Lord, you have seen the times when I've been abandoned by those in whose love I have trusted. You have known the loneliness in my soul. I must confess to you that it causes me to wonder if your love has failed me, too. I need you to assure me that you are still here and that you will always stay with me.

31

For thou hast made him most blessed for ever: thou hast
made him exceeding glad with thy countenance.
—Psalm 21:6

Lord, I open my eyes and all I see are the amazing blessings
that surround me. In this moment, I want for nothing, and I
live with the knowledge that I can always turn to you for help,
and cast my cares upon you, when my clarity and my vision
cloud with worry. Thank you, Lord, for reminding me that
the joyful blessings of this moment are all because of your
love for me.

32

Be still, and know that I am God: I will be exalted among the
heathen, I will be exalted in the earth.
—Psalm 46:10

Lord, it often happens that you are trying to communicate an
important truth to us, but we are so busy searching for the
truth elsewhere that we don't stop and listen. Teach us the
importance of being still, Lord. Only when we are still can we
be aware of your presence and hear your voice. Only when
we quiet the stirrings of our own souls can we connect with
your will! Speak to us, Lord—and help us be ready to listen.

33

God is our refuge and strength, a very present help in trouble.
—Psalm 46:1

Lord, we understand that there are and will be problems in our lives, but please remind us of your presence when the problems seem insurmountable. We want to believe that you know best. We hope to remain patient as we search for purpose. Amen.

34

But let patience have her perfect work, that ye may be perfect and entire, wanting nothing.
—James 1:4

O Lord, what a comfort it is to know that you are working to perfect us even on days when we feel anything but perfect. One day all creation will be perfected. How we look forward to that day when our faith is fully realized, and we are complete in you!

35

He that is of a proud heart stirreth up strife: but he that putteth his trust in the Lord shall be made fat.
—Proverbs 28:25

Lord, we live in a world where there is a great clamoring for power and glory. Greed runs rampant, and time and again we see the inglorious results of someone's unethical attempts to climb to the top. Protect us from such fruitless ambition, Lord. For we know that it is only when we humble ourselves that you will lift us up higher than we could ever have imagined. All power and glory is yours, forever and ever. Until we acknowledge that truth, we will never be great in anyone's eyes—especially yours.

36

Lay not up for yourselves treasures upon earth, where moth and rust doth corrupt, and where thieves break through and steal: But lay up for yourselves treasures in heaven, where neither moth nor rust doth corrupt, and where thieves do not break through nor steal.
—Matthew 6:19–20

O Lord, how many distractions there are in this world! How easy it is for us to get caught up in the desire to acquire, moving from one purchase to the next. How tempting to read one self-help book after another, until we are dizzy. Lord, I know that true contentment, true beauty, and true wisdom are all found only in your Word. Protect me from focusing too much on material things.

37

Blessed are the peacemakers: for they shall be called the children of God.
—Matthew 5:9

Father, you are the greatest of all peacemakers. You made reconciliation with humanity possible by means of great personal sacrifice yet without compromising the truth. Show me how to follow your example today. Help me not to settle for fake peace—the kind that comes when lies are allowed to prevail for the sake of avoiding conflict. Instead, grant me the courage, grace, and wisdom to work toward real peace, which values all people and fulfills our need for truth and love.

38

For, lo, he that formeth the mountains, and createth the wind, and declareth unto man what is his thought, that maketh the morning darkness, and treadeth upon the high places of the earth, The Lord, The God of hosts, is his name.
—Amos 4:13

Lord, we praise you for all the beauty and wonder you've placed in the world. How creative of you to think of a creature as exuberant and joyful as the hummingbird! How interesting that you sprinkled spots on the backs of the newborn fawns that follow along behind their mother through our backyard. Let us never become so accustomed to your glorious creation that we take it for granted, Lord. You've blessed us with a wonderland, and we thank you for it.

39

Delight thyself also in the Lord: and he shall give thee the desires of thine heart.
—Psalm 37:4

Lord, I'm glad that the more I give, the more you give. Reward me for the risks I take on your behalf. Amen.

40

The Lord is my shepherd; I shall not want.
He maketh me to lie down in green pastures: he leadeth me beside the still waters.
—Psalm 23:1–2

Lord, bring me to the place where peace flows like a river, where soft green grasses gently hold the weight of my tired body, where the light of a new sunrise casts warmth.

41

According as his divine power hath given unto us all things that pertain unto life and godliness, through the knowledge of him that hath called us to glory and virtue.
—2 Peter 1:3

Father God, you are the giver of all gifts. All of our resources and all we have came from you, and they are only ours for a little while. Protect us from any addiction to material things, Lord. Gently remind us when we have enough—enough to eat, enough to wear, enough to enjoy. Most of all, keep us mindful of the fact that because we have you, we have everything we need.

42

For thou art great, and doest wondrous things: thou art
God alone.
—Psalm 86:10

My Creator, blessed is your presence. For you and you alone
give me power to walk through dark valleys into the light
again. You and you alone give me hope when there seems
no end to my suffering. You and you alone give me peace
when the noise of my life overwhelms me. I ask that you
give this same power, hope, and peace to all who know
discouragement, that they, too, may be emboldened and
renewed by your everlasting love. Amen.

43

Abide in me, and I in you. As the branch cannot bear fruit of itself, except it abide in the vine; no more can ye, except ye abide in me.
—John 15:4

Lord, I deeply desire to abide in you. I desire to have you abiding in me as well, so closely that I can speak to you any time and feel your presence. Destroy the distractions that create distance between us, Lord. Clear out the clutter that keeps me from sensing your best plan for my life. Then when I ask for what I wish, it will be the fulfillment of your desire for me as well.

44

Even there shall thy hand lead me, and thy right hand shall
hold me.
—Psalm 139:10

I see a robin's egg hatching, Lord, and am set free from my
doubts and fretting. For, while life is not always filled with joy
and happiness, I know it is always held in your hand.

45

Casting all your care upon him; for he careth for you.
—1 Peter 5:7

When trouble strikes, we're restored by the smallest gestures
from God's ambassadors: friends, random kindnesses, shared
pain and support, even a stranger's outstretched hand. And
we get the message: God cares.

46

No man hath seen God at any time. If we love one another, God dwelleth in us, and his love is perfected in us.
—1 John 4:12

O Lord, your gift of love is often distorted in this world of ours. You are the source of the only perfect love we will ever know. Thank you, Lord, for abiding in us and helping us love ourselves and others. On this day, Lord, I pray that you will draw near to anyone who is feeling unloved. May they accept your unconditional love so they will know what true love is!

47

But the scripture hath concluded all under sin, that the promise by faith of Jesus Christ might be given to them that believe.
—Galatians 3:22

Lord, today I want to praise you for giving me the faith to believe, for faith itself is a gift from you. I lift up to you today all those I know who are having trouble accepting your gift of salvation. Be patient with them, Lord. Reveal yourself to them in a way that will reach them, and draw them into a relationship with you. Our lives are incomplete without you, Lord. Send your grace to those who are struggling.

48

Wealth gotten by vanity shall be diminished: but he that
gathereth by labour shall increase.
—Proverbs 13:11

I thank you for my work, Lord. And please bless me in it.
Most of all, help me to remember that the paycheck worth
working for consists of more than just money. It must include
meaning and significance, for myself and others.

49

Jesus answered and said unto him, Verily, verily, I say unto
thee, Except a man be born again, he cannot see the kingdom
of God.
—John 3:3

Spiritual birth is amazing, Father! It's a miracle no less
exciting than the birth of a baby. Your Word says that it
causes even the angels in heaven to rejoice. Thank you for
my own spiritual birth. It's the reason I'm praying right now
and enjoying this fellowship with you. It's so good to be your
child. Today I'll just bask in that reality.

50

The Lord is my strength and song, and he is become my salvation: he is my God, and I will prepare him an habitation; my father's God, and I will exalt him.
—Exodus 15:2

Dear Father God, you sent your son to us to be our Lord, to watch over us, to bring us comfort, strength, hope, and healing, when our hearts are broken and our lives seem shattered. We will never be alone, not when you are here with us always and forever. Remind us to look to you for strength. Amen.

51

Look upon mine affliction and my pain; and forgive all my sins.
—Psalm 25:18

Lord, today I pray for all those who are suffering from any
sort of addiction. Whether it's drugs, gambling, overeating,
or compulsive exercising, Lord, addiction keeps them from
being the people you designed them to be. Their obsession
separates them from you and walls them off from their loved
ones as well. Break through and release them from their
chains, Lord. Give them the strength to put their troubles
behind them and find new life in you.

52

Beloved, now are we the sons of God, and it doth not yet appear what we shall be: but we know that, when he shall appear, we shall be like him; for we shall see him as he is.
—1 John 3:2

Lord, if my hunger and thirst for your righteousness could be satisfied by ordering from a spiritual drive-thru, I'd want to supersize my order! I so want to be like Christ. I want to have his courage and humility, his strength and gentleness. I don't want substitutes—such as pride that looks like courage or fear that looks like humility. I want the real deal. Thank you for the promise that you will satisfy this craving of mine, this deep soul hunger to be and do all that is right, true, and good.

53

I, even I, am he that blotteth out thy transgressions for mine own sake, and will not remember thy sins.
— Isaiah 43:25

A chart of my efforts to change traces a jagged course, Lord, like the lines on a heart-rate monitor. Reassure me that instead of measuring my failures, I must remember that I am alive and ever-changing. Help me become consistent, but deliver me from flat lines.

54

And let the peace of God rule in your hearts, to the which also ye are called in one body; and be ye thankful.
— Colossians 3:15

Sometimes we believe our souls can only be at peace if there is no outer turmoil. The wonder of God's peace is that even when the world around us is in confusion and our emotions are in a whirl, underneath it all we can know his peace.

55

Study to shew thyself approved unto God, a workman that needeth not to be ashamed, rightly dividing the word of truth.
—2 Timothy 2:15

I know it is important to be physically healthy and strong, but how much the better if we're also spiritually strong! Sure, lifting weights does our bodies good, but regularly picking up a Bible is good for the health of our souls. And rather than just doing deep knee bends to increase our physical strength, we can also regularly "hit our knees" in prayer to strengthen our core spirits.

56

Drop down, ye heavens, from above, and let the skies pour down righteousness: let the earth open, and let them bring forth salvation, and let righteousness spring up together; I the Lord have created it.
—Isaiah 45:8

Lift up your heart in sweet surrender to the God who is waiting to shower you with blessings. Lift up your soul on wings of joy to the God who is waiting to guide you from the chaos of shadows out into the light of a peace that knows no equal.

57

I am Alpha and Omega, the beginning and the end, the first
and the last.
—Revelation 22:13

You are everywhere, Lord, and we are comforted to be
enfolded as we move through our lives. You are with us in
birthings and dyings, in routine and surprise, and in stillness
and activity. We cannot wander so far in any direction that
you are not already there.

58

For to be carnally minded is death; but to be spiritually
minded is life and peace.
—Romans 8:6

Spirit, carry me like a feather upon the current to a place of
serenity. Let the waters flow over me like cleansing balm. Set
me upon the dry place, where life begins anew. Spirit, carry
me like a feather back home again.

59

Then came Peter to him, and said, Lord, how oft shall my brother sin against me, and I forgive him? till seven times? Jesus saith unto him, I say not unto thee, Until seven times: but, Until seventy times seven.
—Matthew 18:21–22

Dear God, thank you for children who teach us to be open and forgiving. Help us forgive those who hurt us so the pain will not be passed on through the generations. Thank you for forgiving our sins and help us be at peace with our families. Amen.

60

Serve the Lord with gladness: come before his presence
with singing.
—Psalm 100:2

To serve means to assist or be of use. Serving is one of the
reasons we are on this earth and the reason Jesus himself said
he came to the earth. When we serve, we reach out to meet
the needs of others; service is an outward sign that we belong
to God and desire to do his will. True service is not about
grudgingly doing for others because of obligation, but an act
that flows willingly, as a channel for God's love. True servants
give not just with their hands, but with their hearts. Heavenly
Father, grant me a spirit of true service.

61

And he changeth the times and the seasons: he removeth
kings, and setteth up kings: he giveth wisdom unto the wise,
and knowledge to them that know understanding.
—Daniel 2:21

Just when I settle in with one reality, something new disrupts
it. Overnight change, God of all the time in the world, is
comforting and grief-making, for it's a reminder that nothing
stays the same. Not tough times, not good ones either. Despite
today's annoyance, I'm grateful for change, assured it will take
me to new moments you have in mind.

62

And Abraham said, My son, God will provide himself a lamb for a burnt offering: so they went both of them together.
—Genesis 22:8

One of the Hebrew names for God is Jehovah Jireh. Besides having a nice ring to it, its meaning ("God, our provider") is one worth remembering. In life, we may experience times of abundance and also times when we struggle to make ends meet. In any situation, God asks us to trust and honor him as Jehovah Jireh, the God who provides all that we truly need.

63

Let all bitterness, and wrath, and anger, and clamour, and evil speaking, be put away from you, with all malice.
—Ephesians 4:31

God, grant me the courage to let go of shame, guilt, and anger. Free me of all negative energies, for only then will I become a conduit for joy and a channel for goodness. Amen.

64

Hold up my goings in thy paths, that my footsteps slip not.
—Psalm 17:5

Lord, far too often we try to steer the course of our lives without consulting you, and we always run into problems. Set us on a true course that will bring us closer to you. Amen.

65

God thundereth marvellously with his voice; great things doeth he, which we cannot comprehend.
—Job 37:5

Lord, you come to us in the storm, the fire, and even in the stillness of a quiet moment. Sometimes your message is strong, carried on bustling angelic wings; sometimes our spirits are nudged, our hearts lightened by the gentle whisper of spirit voices. However you approach us, your message is always one of tender love and compassion. Thank you for the certainty—and the surprise—of your holy voice.

66

The thief cometh not, but for to steal, and to kill, and to destroy: I am come that they might have life, and that they might have it more abundantly.
—John 10:10

Father, this morning I woke up, and the gift of life was still within me. What a privilege! I don't want to lose wonder of it for even one day. So help me to live with purpose and joy, not waiting for what today might bring me, but rather looking for opportunities to be and do all that you've created me for. And, most of all, thank you for being with me in each moment, showing me the way of abundant living.

67

Dost thou know when God disposed them, and caused the light of his cloud to shine?
Dost thou know the balancings of the clouds, the wondrous works of him which is perfect in knowledge?
—Job 37:15–16

Nothing thrills the heart and awakens the spirit like a summer thunderstorm, alive with electric energy and thick with potential danger. With each explosive boom of thunder and blinding flash of lightning, our adrenaline rises and our hair stands on end. Without a reminder of our deep connection to the natural world, we can grow dull and lifeless, stiff and anxious, lost and uncertain. Then the thunder roars and the lightning pierces the dark sky, and we remember once again that we are all a part of something far grander and more awesome than we could ever imagine.

68

Watch ye, stand fast in the faith, quit you like men, be strong.
—1 Corinthians 16:13

Even in our toughest moments, Lord, we yearn to grow into fullest flower. Give us a faith as resilient and determined as dandelions pushing up through cracks in the pavement.

69

I will extol thee, O Lord; for thou hast lifted me up, and hast not made my foes to rejoice over me.
—Psalm 30:1

God, when life feels like a ride that won't let us off, remind us that you are waiting for us to reach up to you. And when we finally do, we will thank you for being there to lift us to peace and safety.

70

For the Lamb which is in the midst of the throne shall feed them, and shall lead them unto living fountains of waters: and God shall wipe away all tears from their eyes.
—Revelation 7:17

Lord, how precious water is to us, and how parched and desperate we are when it's in short supply. How grateful we are that in you we have access to the living water that will never run dry! Keep us mindful of that refreshing supply today, Lord. Fill us up, for we are thirsty.

71

Be strong and of a good courage, fear not, nor be afraid of them: for the Lord thy God, he it is that doth go with thee; he will not fail thee, nor forsake thee.
—Deuteronomy 31:6

Dear Lord, each night the news is full of trouble. So much pain and sorrow. It makes me ache to see it all. Some nights, it seems that's all there is; this world seems sometimes so weary and heavy laden. Then I turn to you and know that you are nearest on the darkest days. And there is comfort in knowing you and that you have not forsaken us or the people whose world is presently dark. Amen.

72

Every day will I bless thee; and I will praise thy name for ever and ever.
—Psalm 145:2

The dawn of a new day brings new possibilities and challenges. We hope they'll all be good ones, but we know they won't, and that's where God comes in.

73

And God shall wipe away all tears from their eyes; and there shall be no more death, neither sorrow, nor crying, neither shall there be any more pain: for the former things are passed away.
—Revelation 21:4

I'd like to pray to be spared of all pain, but life is full of pain. No one escapes it. Better to ask God to be near whenever it comes.

74

O give thanks unto the Lord; for he is good; for his mercy endureth for ever.
—1 Chronicles 16:34

Gratitude may be the most underestimated virtue. We think of love, hope, faith, and the power of prayer and forgiveness. But how often do we stop each day and give thanks for all the blessings in our lives? Are we too focused on what we lack, what we don't have, don't want, don't need? By opening the heart and mind to focus on gratitude, we unleash a treasure of unceasing good that's just waiting to flow into our lives. A grateful person knows that by giving thanks, they're given even more to be thankful for. Holy Spirit, open my heart and mind to gratitude for your gifts.

75

And this is the confidence that we have in him, that, if we ask any thing according to his will, he heareth us.
—1 John 5:14

The best listeners are often silent, the depth of their understanding revealed by their actions. God, you are one such listener. Thank you.

76

Grace, mercy and peace from God the Father and from Jesus Christ, the Father's Son, will be with us in truth and love.
—2 John 1:3

Lord, I'm glad you are merciful and gracious. Today I'm resting in your steadfast love, and in your hugs. Amen.

77

For thy mercy is great above the heavens: and thy truth
reacheth unto the clouds.
—Psalm 108:4

His love is wider than our worries, longer than our loneliness,
stronger than our sorrows, deeper than our doubts, and
higher than our hostilities. This is why valleys are so wide,
rivers so long, winds so strong, oceans so deep, and the sky is
so high—with these, we can have a picture of the wonder of
his love.

78

For where two or three are gathered together in my name, there am I in the midst of them.
—Matthew 18:20

Lord, I often pray for others when I need to pray with others. Show me the power of shared prayer as I meet with others in your name and in your presence. Amen.

79

I said, Days should speak, and multitude of years should teach wisdom.
—Job 32:7

Dear God, help me see that aging, like being born, happens one day at a time. Calm my fears that it will overtake and overwhelm me. Help me briefly mourn youth as only a butterfly cocoon that must crumble to set the new creature free.

80

Awake up, my glory; awake, psaltery and harp: I myself will awake early.
—Psalm 57:8

Lord, thank you for being a God of new beginnings. Give me a fresh start today as I trust in you. Amen.

81

Take fast hold of instruction; let her not go: keep her; for she is thy life.
—Proverbs 4:13

Teachers are like gardeners—planting seeds of discovery, cultivating curiosity, and nuturing the joy of learning. Lord, as another school year beckons, I thank you for all who have been good teachers to me and to the children in my life.

82

And be ye kind one to another, tenderhearted, forgiving one another, even as God for Christ's sake hath forgiven you.
—Ephesians 4:32

Dear heavenly Father, I truly want to do good toward others. I don't want to just talk about being good. I desire to be more compassionate. God, I need for you to teach me to be far more sensitive to the needs and sorrows of the people you have placed in my life and to be kind and encouraging toward them. I need for you to teach me how to truly love. I pray for this with all my heart. Amen.

83

And Jesus went about all the cities and villages, teaching in their synagogues, and preaching the gospel of the kingdom, and healing every sickness and every disease among the people.
—Matthew 9:35

Loving Jesus, healer of the sick, I place in your hands myself and all who need your healing, in body or spirit. Help us crave the healing that only you can give. May we not define what that healing should be, but accept your gift of abundant life however you give it to us. In your way, in your time, restore us to full health and wholeness. Amen.

84

For I say, through the grace given unto me, to every man that is among you, not to think of himself more highly than he ought to think; but to think soberly, according as God hath dealt to every man the measure of faith.
—Romans 12:3

Good morning, Lord. I have another busy day ahead of me. This may be the only minute I have to talk to you. Please tap me on the shoulder now and then—no matter how busy I am—and remind me that the world does not revolve around me.

85

They helped every one his neighbour; and every one said to his brother, Be of good courage.
—Isaiah 41:6

I thank you for the healing power of friends and for the positive emotions friendship brings. Thank you for sending companions to me so we can support and encourage one another and share our joys and sorrows. My friends represent for me your presence and friendship here on earth. Please keep them in your care, Father. We need each other, and we need you. Amen.

86

So that we may boldly say, The Lord is my helper, and I will not fear what man shall do unto me.
—Hebrews 13:6

I know there is so much going on in the world that requires your attention. It's just that sometimes I feel tension simply getting a grip on me. Sometimes worry clouds my view. This distances me from you and from everything in my life. I pray for the freedom to worry less. I want to simply trust you more.

87

Let your light so shine before men, that they may see your good works, and glorify your Father which is in heaven.
—Matthew 5:16

Some prayers are best left unfinished, God of abundance, and this will be an ongoing conversation between us. Each day I discover new gifts you offer me, and the list of reasons to be thankful grows. As I accept your gifts and live with them thankfully, guide me to become a person who shares with others so that they, too, can live abundantly. May someone, somewhere, someday say of me, "I am thankful to have this person in my life."

88

For if ye forgive men their trespasses, your heavenly Father
will also forgive you.
—Matthew 6:14

When we truly forgive those who have wronged us, we feel as
light as angel's wings and as free as a child at recess. Heavenly
Father, help me to forgive.

89

Iron sharpeneth iron; so a man sharpeneth the countenance of
his friend.
—Proverbs 27:17

God, you have given me friends to illuminate my path and
make it smooth. They guide me when I am lost and support me
when I stumble. Thank you for bringing them into my life.

90

In that he saith, A new covenant, he hath made the first old. Now that which decayeth and waxeth old is ready to vanish away.
—Hebrews 8:13

Lord, the familiar is disappearing from neighborhood and nature, and we grieve the loss. Yet, we're resurrection people, unafraid of endings because of the promise of beginnings. On the other hand, we must learn restraint: Help us, God, to temper our actions with wisdom. Amen.

91

For the word of God is quick, and powerful, and sharper than any twoedged sword, piercing even to the dividing asunder of soul and spirit, and of the joints and marrow, and is a discerner of the thoughts and intents of the heart.
—Hebrews 4:12

We are, as the Psalmist says, wondrously made. So much so, loving Creator, that by changing our minds we might be able to change our lives. It's the simple power of "as if." Living as if we are going to fail, we often do. Living as if we are going to succeed, we often can. Keep us from being like teams who know the plays but doubt they can run them. Instead, we'll use your amazing gift of attitude, knowing you treat us as if we deserve your promised abundant life.

92

For our conversation is in heaven; from whence also we look for the Saviour, the Lord Jesus Christ.
—Philippians 3:20

When we grieve for lost loved ones, we grieve for ourselves. God, let me celebrate those who have gone home to Heaven, those who now know the full essence of your true love.

93

The word which God sent unto the children of Israel, preaching peace by Jesus Christ: (he is Lord of all).
—Acts 10:36

Love is an active force. When we "walk our talk" and live God's message of love, we create an America full of faith. When we do that, we are God's voice, his hands, his light for each other. We are living love.

94

Therefore being justified by faith, we have peace with God through our Lord Jesus Christ:
By whom also we have access by faith into this grace wherein we stand, and rejoice in hope of the glory of God.
—Romans 5:1–2

Spirit, help me live one day at a time so that I may meet each day's challenges with grace, courage, and hope. Shelter me from the fears of the future and the anguish of the past. Keep my mind and heart focused on the present, where the true gift of happiness and healing is to be found. Amen.

95

And now abideth faith, hope, charity, these three; but the greatest of these is charity.
—1 Corinthians 13:13

The angel of faith helps us trust God despite our circumstance. The angel of hope helps us press on through our circumstance. But the angel of God's love holds us in our circumstance.

96

And when ye stand praying, forgive, if ye have ought against any: that your Father also which is in heaven may forgive you your trespasses.
—Mark 11:25

Father, I need to understand that forgiveness is not dependent on my feelings but rather on a determination of my will. Help me form a few well-chosen words of forgiveness. Amen.

97

Every good gift and every perfect gift is from above, and cometh down from the Father of lights, with whom is no variableness, neither shadow of turning.
—James 1:17

How good it is, Almighty One, to bask in the warmth of your love. How good it is to know nothing more is required than this: to receive your good gifts from above.

98

So that contrariwise ye ought rather to forgive him, and comfort him, lest perhaps such a one should be swallowed up with overmuch sorrow.
—2 Corinthians 2:7

Father, when we stand to cross the metaphorical bridge of forgiveness, please give us a little push to get us going. Amen.

99

Withhold not thou thy tender mercies from me, O Lord: let thy lovingkindness and thy truth continually preserve me.
—Psalm 40:11

Everything around me keeps changing, Lord. Nothing lasts. My relationships with others are different than they were before. I started to feel as if there is nothing sure and steady on which I can depend. Then I remembered your ever-present, unchanging love. Through these transitions, your love gives me courage and hope for the future. Amen.

100

This is a faithful saying, and worthy of all acceptation, that Christ Jesus came into the world to save sinners; of whom I am chief.
—1 Timothy 1:15

Help me, God, to see that you gave your love in such a way that even the most wicked person can repent and find new life in your grace and mercy; indeed, that your love calls even the worst sinners to become your children. You created each person with a specific purpose to serve in this world. Help me, Lord, to pray that each person will turn away from evil, turn to you, and become your devoted servant. Amen.